The Playbook for Success

BY

Amy Broghamer

Ordering Information:

Quantity sales. Special discounts are available on quantity purchases by corporations, associations, and others. Orders by U.S. trade bookstores and wholesalers. Please contact AMY BROGHAMER www.amyb.com.

Edited and Marketed By
DreamStarters University
www.DreamStartersUniversity.com

AMY BROGHAMER

Table of Contents

Support for Playbook for Success

"In life, it's rare to come across a person that walks the talk and has a heart for other people's success as big as Amy B's! She puts the cookies low enough on the shelf that any new or experienced agent can accelerate their growth using her strategies. She's a go-getter and someone we can all learn from!"

-Tim Davis, Author, Speaker and Founder of Personal Branding Mastery

"I have had the honor of coaching thousands of agents all over North America over the years and every once in a while, you meet someone that you know will do great things. Ever since I met Amy, she has stood out as one of those people. Her passion for a systematic approach of delivering a high-level customer experience has allowed her to build a sought-after referral-based business. With her speaking, programs and courses, Amy has been able to give agents that choose to apply her training an unfair advantage in business and life. I'm thankful to have called her a client, business partner, and more importantly, a friend."

- Hank Avink, Founder National Coaching League, Real Estate Coach

"I've enjoyed watching Amy B. continuously bring tremendous value to not only her clients, but also to the real estate community as a whole for a few years now. She shares in a very authentic way, her vast array of knowledge on multiple different subjects. I was so honored that she made the big announcement on my podcast about her book launch. Without a doubt *Playbook for Success* is going to impact and touch tens of thousands of lives for the better. I'm honored to call her a friend and a fellow realtor."
- Greg McDaniel, Realtor and Co-Founder of Real Estate Uncensored Podcast

"Amy is a CATALYST*! Her book will engage you, entertain you, but most of all, educate you. Amy is honest and direct, but most of all, authentic. She studies, practices, and teaches the NET LIFE. I have always appreciated Amy's approach to success, real estate, and life and now she shares her immense wisdom and experience with you. Appreciate her generosity."
-Michael J Maher, two-time bestselling author including the #1 book in Real Estate Sales on Amazon.com, (7L) The Seven Levels of Communication, founder of the Generosity Generation, and CEO of REFERCO, the world's foremost authority in business referrals.

Acknowledgements

I would like to thank and recognize the following people for their contribution to me and by extension, their contribution to this book.

To my parents, Mom and Dad, thank you for providing for me and for leading me by example my whole life. You allowed me to listen to the adult conversations concerning financing and real estate and ask questions, and you educated me on how the world works. You encouraged me and helped me buy my first home at age 19, taught me what it meant to be mindful of finances and credit, and you taught me how to invest in the market, real estate and myself. You showed me the importance and value of having an education. Although I was discouraged from attending college by counselors, you pushed to get me there. You helped me to understand and formulate my big "why," which is to fund my boys' education so they can graduate and begin their lives with the best possible start, just like you gave to me. Those college funds are one of the primary drivers for this book, and my other business endeavors to this day. Thank you, Mom and Dad, for your influence and encouragement to be and do anything I want—I am doing it!

To my husband, Steve, the best decision I ever made was to be your partner. Looking back with some perspective, there aren't enough ways for me to thank you for being my equal in life and business. And for being just as cool with letting me lead and you follow, as you are with leading yourself. Thank you for always being honest with me about my ideas, for helping me think through my plans, for encouraging me to always push through, and for showing our boys what it means to be a father that respects their mother and treats everyone with respect and equality.

To my kids, thanks for all of the endless lessons on negotiation, perseverance, and not taking no for an answer. You two are ruthless. You guys are my life's greatest challenge and greatest pride. Your encouragement of my writing this book was both surprising and persistent, and I am grateful for your interest in my success and happiness. I can only hope you both stay on the wonderful path you are both on today and that you encourage each other's success and happiness always.

To my friend, Anne, thank you for your serendipitous interest, encouragement, and support while writing this book. The timing has been terrific, along with so many life lessons learned between us in the last year from some of the very same concepts in this book. Thank you for being on this journey with me and taking this book full-circle. I can't wait to return the favor in your next adventure.

To my business partner and buyer specialist, Jenny. I appreciate your support and encouragement for our real estate business and all of these fun side projects that I do. I'm grateful for the commitment you have to our real estate clients, your focus on what is best for them and your outstanding and unwavering integrity.

To my mentor and friend, Hank. Thank you for always being honest with me and for your wisdom and encouragement over the years. Thanks for helping me see the big picture when it wasn't obvious to me, and for that famous headlock. You inspire me to continue to share the concepts of a Net Life and to live it with intention every day. Your impact has already caused significant positive ripples that will continue to enrich my Net Life for many years.

To my friend and inspiration, Tim Davis. Thank you for supplying me with the spark and motivation that caused me to take action and write a book. It was YOU that told me anyone could write a book, and that there are no rules, no required number of chapters, length or font size! Thank you for your friendship and sharing yourself with so many. Go Cats!

To my friend, author Michael Maher. You signed my *7L* book, and I cherish that to this day. Knowing and following you for the last 10 years has been a wonderful experience.

To my financial advisor, Jason Harsh. By merely helping us as a newly married couple with our budget and reserves, YOU helped create a confidence in me that you cannot even begin to understand. You and your guidance and perseverance enabled us to find our own success with our finances, our savings and our retirement. You have set us up for success today and in the future, and we are endlessly grateful.

I would also like to thank the band Pearl Jam, for being there for me since 1991 to modern day. Many years in between, when my career, business and family took priority, I lost you, and some of my Net Life as a result. Thank you for continuing to make music, for speaking your mind and heart to your audience, and for continuing to TOUR. Now that I have a focus on my Net Life again, I will be in attendance at your shows as often as possible for the rest of my life.

Thank you to Oprah Winfrey for being an example of a healthy, intelligent, generous and inspiring woman. You have shown the world that anything is possible and what it looks like to be responsible for yourself and your own destiny. I sobbed the day your show ended, and a few times since, yet I know you are living your best life in your next phase and that challenge and passion is also terribly inspiring to me.

Special thanks to Jamie Hurtubise, Jesy and George Herron, Dawn Loding, the Anderson Township Fire Department, Marcella's Doughnuts and Bakery, Chris McClure, Nancy Walton, Mike Fallat, Counsel of Residential Specialists, Keller Williams Realty and EXP Realty, Lead Gen Scrips and Objections Group, Real Estate Uncensored, The National Coaching League, all of my Master Listing Specialists and Expert Buyers Specialists.

Introduction

Why Playbook for Success?

In gathering my ideas and thoughts to write and in starting the process of writing and editing, I came to believe that what has been included in this book are many of the key pieces for setting yourself up for success. This book is based on stories, and it's based on mistakes I have made and the lessons I have learned from those mistakes that ultimately elevated me to success. It contains a running list of potential traps that could cause failure, tips on how to not get caught in them and a game plan for how to position yourself to succeed, and WIN! I found myself using the phrase "game plan" to describe each lesson, which is a phrase I use in my daily life, so I decided this book should be considered a playbook. Each chapter will give you a game plan to WIN!

What is success? Throughout this book I use the term success quite a bit. So, right now, I want to take the time to explain, before you begin reading, what my definition of the word success is, because it's probable that your definition is different.

My definition of success is broader in scope than successful completion of a task; success is often defined as the accomplishment of a specific aim or purpose. I believe true success is only accomplished when it is experienced in both business and in life.

Success means having a thriving business. One that is healthy, has a positive energy, does rewarding and quality work, and creates positive results and satisfied customers. Success means having a business that's financially healthy, with realistic and repeatable profits resulting from reasonable work hours.

Success also means having a rewarding life outside of the work you do—reasonable work hours define your business, and the rest of the time is there for you to create a life you enjoy. Having the time to create a life outside of work, to live that life and to enjoy that life, with friends, family and children, is the other half of what I mean by success when I refer to it in this book. While balancing these two parts is often a constant challenge, I have attempted to share with you some game plans that I believe, with practice, will get you closer to the balance that is success.

We work to live, we don't live to work.

Let me introduce you to the idea of NET LIFE, a concept championed by my friend and mentor, Hank Avink. This idea of NET LIFE is what I wish for everyone reading this book to achieve. It is closely aligned with my definition of success above. NET LIFE, to me, means you are able to enjoy financial security with your business, freedom with your work to do what is your passion, and quality relationships with people that are your friends and family. To me, that's living your best life. That's what I want for myself, and for everyone I encounter.

The reality is, so few people have this NET LIFE. So few have the conviction or often the tools or the knowledge of how to obtain their best NET LIFE. It is my hope that this book will move everyone that reads it to take a few steps closer to their best life, whatever that may be for you.

That brings us to the game plan! Just as every sports team has a playbook, with many different ideas and plans that all lead to them winning, this book will guide you to create your own game plan for success. At the end of each chapter, you will find a game plan for you to take action on. The game plan includes questions to think about, action items to tackle and practice exercises to complete. Those who take no action will get beat, those execute will WIN! Which are you? This book, and all that is included, provides you with the opportunity to create your own personalized *Playbook for Success.* Take action, execute the plan and WIN YOUR NET LIFE!

Everyone works, everyone has a life. It's how you live it that matters, so why wait? Start living your best life now!

Onward

Inspiration

"If we did all the things we are capable of doing, we would literally astound ourselves."

Thomas A. Edison

"Our deepest fear is not that we are inadequate. Our deepest fear is that we are powerful beyond measure. It is our light, not our darkness that most frightens us. We ask ourselves, 'Who am I to be brilliant, gorgeous, talented, and fabulous?' Actually, who are you not to be? You are a child of God. Your playing small does not serve the world. There is nothing enlightened about shrinking so that other people will not feel insecure around you. We are all meant to shine, as children do. We were born to make manifest the glory of God that is within us. It is not just in some of us; it is in everyone and as we let our own light shine, we unconsciously give others permission to do the same. As we are liberated from our own fear, our presence automatically liberates others."

Marianne Williamson

Chapter 1

Do I Have Permission to Be Honest with You?

This book begins with my favorite question: Do I have permission to be honest with you? My friends in the real estate business often come to me when they need to hear the truth. I am happy to be known as someone who isn't afraid to be honest and share my unfiltered opinion. I don't know any other way to be.

There are sometimes negative consequences that come with this. Honesty turns some people off. It terrifies them. I acknowledge that, and I also respect it. Yet it doesn't change what I have to offer to others.

We all operate differently, and we can all learn from each other. That's what this book is all about. It's not about me being your guru or drill sergeant. I've been described as "the tough love realtor" by clients and colleagues. This is because I strive to honestly share what I know will help people succeed with their goals, with as much clarity as possible. If you're serious about having a healthy and thriving real estate business, and you want to be able to sustain your productivity and have a rewarding and present personal life, this book is for you.

It is comprised of the lessons I've learned working as a real estate agent for over a decade. Throughout my time as an agent, I've experienced my fair share of failures and successes. I've gone through a lot of trial and error to get to where I am today. My goal is to help you bypass some of that process and instead focus your attention on the things that really matter in order for you to experience success in the real estate industry.

This book is designed to show you exactly how to get realistic about your business. It's going to give you the fundamentals needed for success that are true across the board. You can think of it as a playbook for how to take care of yourself *and* run a successful business as a real estate agent. Once you understand the "plays," the WINS you can get from applying the things you learn will amaze you.

The one thing you need to have to approach the lessons in this book properly is an open mind and the willingness to implement these things into your own business and life. By continuing to read on, you're giving me permission to be honest with you and show you exactly what needs to be done in order for you to succeed, even if it causes you to be uncomfortable at first.

After all, if you want to get different results than you're currently getting, you're going to have to do something different. As one of my favorite authors, Jack Canfield, says, "Everything you want is on the other side of your comfort zone." This book, in many cases, is going to take you right to that place, so let's get uncomfortable!

The first thing I do when I start working with a new client, is ask them, "Do I have permission to be honest with you?" This is a defining question that causes people to sit up and pay attention, and it truly sets the stage for the rest of the relationship.

When you ask someone for permission to be honest with them, it sets one hell of a precedent and expectation for the relationship from the beginning. The expectation becomes, "I'm going to be honest with you, and you're going to be honest with me." That's a foundation for a successful relationship.

What is great about this is, at any part of the process, you're able to say, "Hey, remember when you gave me permission to be honest with you?" This anchors anything that is said after that.

If you're still reading, I'm going to assume you do want honesty from me in this book, so I'm not going to tell you what you want to hear. For example, I'm not going to tell you that everybody is cut out to be successful in real estate. If it were easy, more people would do it. It's not easy. It's not for everyone. Nothing worth doing or having is easy.

This is why it's important for you to be honest with yourself first and foremost. You have to ask yourself the tough questions and be willing to answer them. Who are you? Is being in business for yourself right for you? You may have a desire to kill it in real estate, but are you being honest with yourself about what it's going to take to do that? Are you prepared to do the work to get there?

You don't have to answer these questions right now, yet if you want reading this book to make a big impact on your business and your life, you have to realize it's not my words that are going to make the difference for you. It's what you do after discovering the answers to those questions that counts.

Not too long after I started in real estate, I was called in to assist a first-time home seller (now dear friend) and her husband in selling their home after they had failed to sell it with another agent. I took them through my process of investigating what they owed on their property, what it would look like to sell it, and how things would play out for them once it was all said and done.

I remember sitting at the kitchen table with them and laying out all the paperwork. I took them through understanding where the values were going to fall—what they owed on their house, what they could expect to get for it, and what money that would leave them with at the end of the day. It was a negative number, and I could tell they were crushed.

This is the unfortunate part about being honest with people. Sometimes it makes them cry. Sometimes it makes them angry with you. All kinds of emotions come up when you're honest. I had to tell this couple, "Listen, I can't sell your house for you. It's not the right thing to do for your family. If you sell it, you're going to need to bring another $15,000 to the table in order to get into another home. If you don't have that, then you'll end up being homeless or living with your parents."

When I told them this, the woman started to cry. It was a massive moment of clarity for her. She said to me, "Oh my God, why didn't the previous agent who listed our house tell us this was going to happen?"

Empathetic, yet confident in my conclusions, all I could say was, "I don't know how other agents run their business. It's very important to me that you know what it's going to look like at the end of the process when we accomplish the goal of selling your house." I knew it didn't make sense for them to sell their house and go down that path right then. I knew it wasn't right for their family, and I told them that.

What happened as a result was they didn't list their house with me that day. Instead, I connected them with a financial planner, an amazing partner of mine who helps people budget, plan and save to be in a position of power.

Three years down the road, the couple called me and said, "We've got that $15,000 we needed, and we're ready to go. Come help us sell our house." Because I was honest and helped this family, they referred me to at least a dozen other friends, family and colleagues over time.

I didn't make any money the day I had to break the news to them that they couldn't sell their house, yet I was able to put them on the path to good things for their future and their family; in return, they delivered continued trust and a positive testimonial to others in their circle.

"I wish I was the messenger, and all the news was good." These are the lyrics to the song "Wish List" by one of the greatest Rock and Roll Hall of Fame bands of all time, Pearl Jam. Those lyrics are always piercing to me when I hear them. They remind me of my responsibility to be honest, no matter what a person's wishes might be that I'm delivering a message to.

As an agent, the news I must deliver to people is not always good. When this is the case, I wish I could tell people something better, but I can't. My wish is that people will respect me enough to deliver the hardest truths, and I can only apply this wish in how I communicate with others. Honesty is the highest form of respect.

Real estate agents are often afraid to give people bad news or say what their clients don't want to hear. They don't want people to associate them with bad news. They think it will mean that people won't call on them for help or hire them.

I find the opposite is true. When you are honest with people, you give them the clarity and understanding required to achieve the success that they seek. Then when they succeed, they appreciate the honesty you shared and know it was the key element they needed to change to pivot their trajectory towards success. Honesty is the foundation of this book, my life and my business.

Game Plan

- ✓ Be honest with yourself first. Reflect and ask yourself, and perhaps even those that know you best:
  - Is being in business for myself right for me?
  - Am I focused enough to do the hard work it takes to meet my goals for business and family with a career in real estate?

- ✓ Start asking for permission to be honest with teammates, partners and clients to set the stage for a successful relationship.

- ✓ Can you set aside your own needs to put the clients' family and financial well-being first?

"Befriend the man who is brutally honest, for honesty is the highest form of respect."

Daniel Saint

Chapter 2

A Mistake Repeated is a Decision

Everything you experience in business is a learning opportunity. The way you receive and respond to what happens to you is how you learn and move forward, either successfully or unsuccessfully. In real estate, you might know of agents that never seem to be able to grow their business and get better at what they do. We often hear this described with the phrase, "They have been having their first year for 10 years." Inside or outside of real estate, failing to improve with experience and failing to acknowledge the changes required to grow is a quick recipe for stagnation.

People who fail to do this are not bettering themselves. They're not utilizing different tools or processes in order to get better. They're simply having the same year, every year. They aren't choosing to build on successes, and they aren't learning from their failures.

You see, as you do business, you're going to make mistakes. This is unavoidable. Things are going to happen that don't go your way, and your job is to learn from those things, and create a solution that causes them to never occur again, and then move on. A mistake repeated is a decision.

Every day in business as a real estate agent you have to make decisions. You have to ask yourself, "Am I going to take on a jerk client? Am I going to take listings in this area? Am I going to continue to work with investment properties?" These are examples of decisions you might have to make. There are so many more.

What it breaks down to is being able to look at your experience and decide, "Do I want to repeat that? Or do I not want that to happen ever again?"

When something that I don't like happens in my business, I always say to myself, "Okay, I made a mistake.

This did not work out well. What can I do in the future to make sure this doesn't happen again?" The answer might be to adjust an approach or a plan, and to put a standard in place to guard against or mitigate the problem and reduce or eliminate the odds of it occurring in the future.

The definition of insanity is doing the same thing and expecting a different result. When something you don't want to happen is continuing to occur, it's important to understand that it's happening because you're making it happen. You're making a decision to let it happen by not diagnosing why it happened in the first place, and not putting a plan in place to keep it from happening again. I'm here to help you avoid insanity and learn from your mistakes.

Early in my career in real estate, I learned a lot of lessons through trial and error. I remember sitting down at my dining room table in December of 2008, and at that time I had been in business as an agent for about three years.

On my table, I had spread out all the listings I had sold that year, and the listings I hadn't sold. I took a really deep look at the listings that weren't selling or failed to sell. 2008 was a year when the real estate market took one of the worst hits in history, and I identified that only some of the problem was the market conditions. However, those market conditions were merely amplifying the lack of processes or the poor strategies and tools we utilized to sell listings. In a way, that terrible market allowed me to see on a large scale, what wasn't working.

I identified the things I did and didn't do that ultimately caused the homes not to sell. When I added up all the sales that didn't happen that I took on that year, I realized how much time I'd spent on them that I didn't get paid for. And it wasn't only time that I'd lost. There were also expenses related to advertising and technology that I didn't recoup.

The worst part to me, was that there were also promises made to people that never came to fruition. There were moms and dads who wanted to move closer to their kids, and they couldn't do that because we couldn't get their houses sold. There were people that lost their jobs and needed to reduce overhead, that we were unable to sell homes for because they were upside down. There were people hoping to fund the down payment for their next home with the equity from their first, yet there was none. The list went on.

On top of all this, when I added up the volume of what could have been sold and looked at what my fee would have been, it was obvious how much money I had left on the table. The reality was I had been spinning my wheels. At the time, I didn't have kids. Two kids and 10 years later, I would be so upset if I was missing soccer games, school plays and dinner at home with my family with nothing to show for it.

I'm glad that on that day in December 2008, I laid everything out on the table and was honest with myself about what I had failed to do and what I could do better. The result was I created the beginning of a system that later became my first online course that focuses on bulletproofing the sale of a home with everything I learned from my mistakes in those early days. The course is called "Sell 100% of Your Listings." What this system allows me to do is make sure my clients and I are on the same page, and that I am able to bulletproof their sale and nearly guarantee success in selling their home.

I designed this system to correct any and all mistakes I had made with the homes that hadn't sold. I'll share my main mistakes, and my solutions along with some of the standards that I chose to set to cause them not to be repeated.

Mistake 1:

Overpricing

At times, and this is often practiced in the industry, I told clients what they wanted to hear in regard to their property's value, and this led to unfulfilled expectations. Other times, I simply didn't know any better, and I priced properties too high. To correct these issues, I had to create a very specific process for pricing a property.

Solution to Overpricing:

My new process investigates price from many angles, giving clarity to both myself and my clients. I discovered that educating the clients on these tools brings clarity and an understanding to them and makes the final strategy and game plan for selling end with a WIN for them.

My Standard:

I always, always, always do my pricing research and I never allow myself to discredit my proven process or their homes value with "guessing" at a value vs. investing the time to research and gather the facts. It is my policy to never "guess" at a home's value, the client deserves better than that.

Mistake 2:
Attracting Buyers

Next, I took a look at what tools and systems I was using to draw buyers in. I had to make sure photos of every property looked great, and that each property was staged to appeal to the most buyers. A huge issue I uncovered was that the homes that didn't display well were simply not selling.

Solution to Attracting Buyers = Presenting the Homes:

I determined that staging, and simply walking a client room by room and making recommendations for exactly what to do to make their home look better, causes a home to photograph better, and allows it to appeal to a wider range of buyers. This needed to be a part of the solution. This caused better photos and for buyers to fall in love before stepping foot into a home, giving the seller a head start!

My Standard:

With every single listing I take, I provide a complete staging report. Every seller is given a written report that provides them with a checklist for creating the absolute BEST presentation for their home. Every single property, no exceptions. The impact of this one tool is great.

Mistake 3:
Property Inspections Were Killing Sales

At the time, and I assume there will always be, a representative amount of homes being "flipped," meaning people were buying an ugly or outdated home and fixing it up, making it look better and then selling it for significantly more money. There were all levels of investors buying homes and flipping them who were also learning as they went. They'd make surface level changes to a home, essentially the equivalent of putting lipstick on a pig, and then ask me to sell it. A pig with lipstick.

There were a bunch of investors who wanted to list their properties with me. And what kept happening was we'd get the property sold, and then we'd go through inspections, and there would be 35 problems on the list that needed fixed before it could close. This scared buyers away.

Solution to Inspection Issues:

To solve this problem, I started requiring investors to have their property inspected before we listed it. As an investor, if you take care of problems before they occur, you tee yourself up for success from the beginning. This will give you a stronger sale price in the end. It's all about profit to an investor, and they saw how this kept their equity high, so they followed my playbook.

In fact, I always tell anyone who is selling a home to take more time upfront to get a property ready to sell. It makes the whole final process smoother and less stressful for everyone.

My Standard:

I strongly encourage every homeowner to get an inspection of their own home before we enter the house on the market, and in most cases, I require a pre-listing inspection. This allows the homeowner to know more about their home than a buyer. It allows any sellers that are tight on funds, to protect their equity, and possibly, pause the sale process if they discover an issue that they cannot afford to correct that would ultimately cost them too much money. It's always the best move for a seller to know more about their property than anyone else.

As a result of the changes I made to my strategy, my listing success rate jumped from 60% to where it is now—100%. Yes, it really is possible to sell and close 100% of your listings if you are honest with clients and yourself and put systems in place. This is why I created **Sell 100% of Your Listings**. In this course, I show you how to make sure you experience no missed opportunities in your business.

One of my favorite quotes from the course is, "Some of the best listings you take are the ones you don't." Even veteran agents sometimes forget that you don't have to take on every client that walks through your door. The most important job you have as a real estate agent is making sure your client is motivated to do what it takes to get their home sold for the most money. If they are unable or unreasonable, and this simply can't be done, it's in everyone's best interest to be honest and not accept the listing.

← Game Plan →

✓ Sit down and reflect upon patterns and decisions you make in your life. Is there a mistake you continue to repeat?

✓ What mistakes have you made in your life and business that you'd like to not repeat again?

✓ What are possible solutions or standards you can put in place to create success next time?

Mistakes lead to creating Rules known as Standards.

Chapter 3

If You Say So!

One of my mentors, Hank Avink, has a saying he likes to use to push back when he encounters limiting beliefs in others. He uses it on the regular, and I get great joy out of using it whenever possible. It's the simple response to a limiting belief or excuse, "If you say so." What we know, is whatever we tell ourselves is true.

As a real estate agent, here is an example of a typical client limiting belief you may have heard a few times, *"I can't sell my house in December. No one buys a house during the holidays."* And we would respond… "If you say so." Then we would go about finding the reasons why people DO buy homes in December. Most corporate hiring and relocations happen at the start of the year, which also happens to be right in the middle of winter. There are plenty of serious people buying and selling homes in the winter, and there are fewer homes to compete with in the winter each year. It's consistently been the strongest season every year for both leads and sales on our team.

I held a limiting belief for many years that *the real estate business and lifestyle wouldn't work for me.* Growing up, I watched my mom sell real estate. She was a top agent, a hard worker and that worked for her! She worked 24/7, and I understood that to mean that in order to be a top producer and make the kind of money I wanted, I would have to give my life to this business.

That was the main reason I resisted getting into real estate for myself for as long as possible. I didn't believe I could succeed in real estate without having to work all the time, including every evening and every weekend.

I didn't believe I could make it work for me without being attached to my phone and on call 24/7. However, by simply being aware that this would be a challenge in my path, I was able to focus on listening for ideas and techniques to create some boundaries. When my "WHY" (my reason for living/working) got big enough, I found solutions for overcoming this limiting belief and created a business in real estate that I love.

The experience I gained through watching my mom perform at a high level in real estate allowed me to have a great head start in the business while also knowing some of the pitfalls that were up ahead. I was empowered to do it my way! It took me a long time to realize that by believing it wasn't possible to be involved in real estate in a completely balanced way, I was limiting my beliefs and my success in real estate.

The truth all along was that I could create a business and lifestyle in real estate, the one I have now, where I work Monday through Friday from 7:30 a.m. to 4:30 p.m. The only time I work in the evening or on a weekend is when it's on my schedule or when I'm negotiating a sale; this is actually quite rare. For a time, while making this schedule transition, my husband would often ask if I was selling any houses, since he had been so used to having me always on the phone in the evenings.

How did I do it? I focused on listings and hired a buyer's agent. If you are a solo agent, you can work with a showing assistant that can do evening and weekend showings. I began to offer to schedule meetings and showings during work hours, and when given two options, clients would choose one, both during the work hours. I prepared clients in advance for how offers work and the best way to prepare and deliver them, and, of course, that's during the workday.

There are so many great tools and tips, things that might be uncomfortable to try at first, yet work out amazingly as you create your ideal work and non-work hours. It is possible for anyone to have a few nights a week off, or even a weekend day or a whole weekend. Don't fool yourself into thinking that's not an option in this business!

Have you ever thought...

"I'll never be able to make 6 figures in real estate."

That was a real limiting belief my buyer's agent had prior to joining my team. Jenny had been in the business for almost 10 years when she joined me. She was looking for a higher income. For the first ten years of her career in real estate, she consistently earned around $40k in gross commissions. This was an example of having the same year over and over. And a true example of what setting standards will do for your income.

Now that Jenny has joined my team and has been introduced to our team standards, she says NO a LOT more than she ever has. And you better believe she was worried about saying NO so much! But guess what happened? She started saying NO, and her income grew and grew and grew! Now, on my team, she was expected to follow my Ultimate Buyer Loyalty Process, which causes more than 95% of buyers that following the process to CLOSE on a house. So, I packaged that right up, and it's now an online course. It's available for any real estate agent to experience the same results.

It's a simple system; our buyers must:

- Get pre-approved by a trusted lender
- Sit down and do a counseling session with us so we can understand what they are looking for and educate them on the process
- Decide to hire our team to represent them

When these three basic items are completed, they will buy a house more than 95% of the time. Jenny implemented the process, which includes a few more tips and tools, and after the first year with our team, her GCI doubled, to $80k. She started saying NO to people that weren't pre-approved, to people that didn't want to commit to hiring her or our team. In her next year with our team, her income increased again to well over the $100k mark. SIX figures!

All this was accomplished by saying NO and forcing herself to set the right standards for her business. As the lead agent of the team, I'm thrilled that we are converting buyer leads at a 95%+ close rate and letting go of the ones that would have ended up taking time away from the best ones. This system has been shared with many agents and team leaders training buyer's agents with similar results. With the right tools, and conviction, you can make 6 figures in real estate!

How about...

"*They won't hire me because I'm too new.*"

You know what... "If you say so." Let's think about what training and experiences you can get quickly so that you can have more experience that leads to your confidence in sharing with a seller or a buyer why they should hire you!

Create a game plan that includes getting the training and experience YOU need to feel confident about sharing with a client that YOU ARE the best fit for their needs. Go out there and find the tools and training you need to set yourself apart and feel confident in the business. And a quick, shameless plug, if you decide to hop into one of my online courses, you will graduate out of there like you OWN the market you are in with the tools, training and systems we give you to use in your business.

We truly have trained brand new agents that were then able to eliminate their more experienced competition with the impressive resources from our **Sell 100% of Your Listings** and **Ultimate Buyer Loyalty Process** programs.

Now, let's game plan on how to conquer these limiting beliefs and WIN! A common problem I see among agents is they don't even know how many houses they want or need to sell. They don't know how much money they want to make. They just want to help people.

There's nothing wrong with wanting to help people, yet to run a successful or profitable real estate business you have to put some numbers to it in order to stay in business and continue to help people. You must have a clear vision of your goals and what you are striving for. If you don't give yourself direction, you will stay trapped in the same place and continue to have your first year for 10 years vs. grow and evolve to the next level. No one else can move you forward. It's all on you.

Do you want to be successful business owner? Do you want to be a successful agent that can fund your family's budget with your income? These were my expectations when I got started in real estate. I wanted to be the breadwinner for my family. That was my goal. In order to accomplish this, I had to believe and say, "I'm going to accomplish this!"

Now, I recognize that some real estate agents choose to only sell a few houses a year, or only use their license when a friend calls to sell a home. This, however, is not the type of career I wanted. I wanted to build a profitable, thriving, full-time, growing real estate business. You and you alone must decide what you want out of your real estate career, and make the commitment.

Do you want to sell homes part-time, only when a friend calls? Or, rather, are you in pursuit of a successful, thriving, growing business that allows you to control your success, income and work life balance? If this is your goal, having clear goals and an end in mind is imperative.

Begin with the end in mind. Write out goals and plans to accomplish those goals from day one. When you decide to believe in yourself, it might look to other people like arrogance, yet you must persist. You have to say, "I'm going to be in the top 1%, and I'm going to sell 50 homes this year." If you don't start with belief in yourself, why should anyone else believe in you?

This is why I believe it's a big mistake if you don't have a vision for where you want to be with your business and what you want to accomplish. You need to have your goals written down, no matter how far-fetched they might seem to you right now. A goal not written down is only a dream. When a goal is written down, you have clarity about it and can start taking the small steps necessary to reach it.

Start there, no matter if it is day one or year 12. Overcome your limiting beliefs with clear goals and plans, and you will create for yourself a successful and profitable business.

Check out a basic and focused game plan in the following image. Keep things simple and focused.

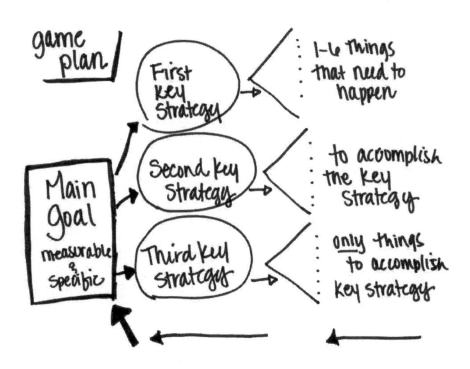

Game Plan

✓ What limiting beliefs do you have in your life and business?

✓ Ask yourself: If you knew you could not fail, what would you do? How would you do it?

✓ Set goals that crush your limiting beliefs, draw up a game plan and go after it with confidence.

BONUS:
Download your Game Plan Template and start overcoming your limiting beliefs at www.amyb.com/gameplan

"If you think you can or you think you can't, you are RIGHT!"

Henry Ford

Chapter 4

Clarity of Vision

In early 2016, I created my first 10-year vision board. I always resisted putting things down on a vision board up to this point. I thought it was silly. When I finally made my first vision board, within six months, half of the board started to come to fruition.

On my board, I had an income goal listed, and I started making great strides towards it. I also put down that I wanted to be a public speaker, and I landed a few speaking engagements. I put down that I wanted to open a new business, and I did. Creating my own book was also on my vision board, and that's how this book you're reading and holding in your hands right now came to be.

When you put something down on a vision board, it holds you accountable to what you've put down. It serves as a constant reminder for what you've set out to do (so make sure it's within view of your office chair, or somewhere else you spend a lot of time). Another way you can hold yourself accountable to your goals is by sharing them with other people.

For example, one of my longer-term goals is to own a house in Hawaii (the Big Island, or next to Eddie Vedder's house!). It's on my vision board, and I have made sure my kids and my husband know that. They see my vision board. We talk about it. It's part of our daily conversation. Our conversations keep me motivated to keep pushing forward towards the goal of making the house a reality.

My family reminds me of my goals because of sharing this vision with them, and this helps me keep the clarity of the vision. If you don't yet have kids, believe me, they NEVER FORGET your promises! They'll hold you accountable more than anyone else can! If you've got kids, you already know, be careful what you tell them, and also, allow them to hold you accountable on a whole new level!

When you have a goal, you have to be able to say to yourself, "I will get there. I am doing this. I am going to be successful." Having conviction is the first step, and the second step is surrounding yourself with the people that believe in you and will help you pursue what you want. This is family, mentors, coaches, trainers and people with good energy that will help fuel you forward.

I feel very fortunate to have always surrounded myself with people who are promoters and not haters. For some people, they get into real estate and even their family tells them they're going to fail.

How many times have you heard that starting your own business is a recipe for disaster? That most businesses and entrepreneurs fail? The general population loves to focus on the failures of others instead of the successes. When you're surrounded by other people that are a negative influence on you and your business, including family, friends and clients, this can really bring you down and block your ability to succeed.

For example, when the housing market crashed in 2008 and foreclosures and short sales were popping up everywhere, people would often say to me, "Things are tough right now, aren't they? Are you getting out of the real estate business? Are you looking for another job? Are you going to go back to selling pharmaceuticals?" It happened then, and I know it'll happen again in the next shift, and I'll be prepared.

When the going gets tough, the tough get going. When the market is down, that's when you need to kick things up a notch, and change and adjust your strategy to make things happen. Bad energy has no place in the life of someone who is determined to continue moving forward regardless of the challenges they are faced with.

I've always been one to eliminate bad energy out of my life. If somebody I've associated with is bringing me down, then it's my responsibility to cut ties with them. I set myself up for success with the good energy that boosts me. I seek out clients, family and friends that have a positive influence to surround and support me and keep my good energy high.

A positive mindset is the most important thing you can have in order to put yourself in a good position mentally for yourself, your clients and your family. When you consciously surround yourself with people who support your vision, goals and energy, it clears the path to you achieving your goals.

I always seek out people, ideas, and solutions that will encourage and inspire me. Your goal should be to bring in as much good into your life as you can. To do that, you have to make room for the good by getting rid of the bad. Please note, bringing in the GOOD takes time and effort!

Even if you don't have direct access to the mentors you'd like to have right now, there are other ways you can absorb their influence. For example, while I'd love to have Oprah Winfrey as a personal friend and mentor, that's not a reality for me at this point. Regardless, I can still learn from her.

I watch her videos, read her articles and books, and I study what she recommends I study. I do this because I know the more I surround myself with things that come from a positive and successful source, the more they will affect my life in a positive way. They say, be careful who you ask for advice from, as you will end up like them. This goes for the good and the bad!

If someone you respect recommends a book to you, it takes time to go get that book, read it and implement its tools and teachings. Regardless, you owe it to yourself to better yourself, and this is one way you can do it.

An amazing thing happens when you invest in yourself. You gain the ability to share what you've learned with the people around you, and then they are better equipped to support you in the future. Over time, the amount of knowledge and wisdom in your circle compounds, and everyone benefits in a miraculous way. This kind of investment no longer yields results by addition, it's now MULTIPLICATION!

What is your vision for your life and business? The whole point of creating a vision for your life, surrounding yourself with positive people and investing in yourself is to live a life you truly love with the people you care about the most. You work to have this life. You don't have this life because you work.

Game Plan

✓ Create a vision board and share it with your cheerleaders (family, co-workers, friends).

✓ Identify cheerleaders in your life that support your vision and game plan. Surround yourself with them often.

✓ Keep a list of things that give you good energy and a spark of positivity—videos, songs, quotes, books, etc.

BONUS:
Get Amy's personal favorite energy boosting videos and sparks at www.amyb.com/sparks

"The only thing worse than being blind is having sight but no vision."

Helen Keller

Chapter 5

Getting Uncomfortable

When the housing market started crashing in 2008, homes were harder to sell. They took longer to sell and close, and they were worth less money. As a result, my average sale price dropped, as did my income.

There were a lot of negatives I could have focused on. Instead I had to ask myself, "What is the good here?" The good was that I had started selling more houses, even though they were worth less money. Another positive was that I was connecting with more people, and I was connecting with them on a deeper level.

The relationships I developed with people during the down market were formulated around me helping them out of often tough situations. By being able to help people in their time of need, there was a bonding experience that happened between us.

I did my best to dig people out of the holes they were in. If being in real estate had been all about the money for me at this time, being able to feel positive about what I was doing would have been difficult. My business is not only about making money. It's about solving problems for clients, and the crash of 2008 and the years that followed created big problems to solve for many.

I knew that by showing commitment to my work, I would foster relationships with clients that would eventually lead to business growth in the future. By investing in relationships during the hard times, I knew the rewards would come later.

Because I was able to help people in a big way, I earned their trust. This led to people recommending me to their friends and family left and right. They were able to say to others, "You've got to work with Amy. She did a great job for us when things were really difficult." This was often even the case when a sale didn't make sense or work out.

Don't get me wrong. Going through a down market as a real estate agent is very difficult. It's extremely uncomfortable, and you don't know when things are going to turn around. Many agents left the business to get back to the comfort of a "normal" job.

Going through such a difficult time period helped me build confidence. In fact, I'm actually ready for it to happen again because I'm confident that I'm going to be able survive and even thrive. This next time around, I will already be an expert in what I need to be doing, and I will be aggressively looking for the challenges and quickly creating solutions for them.

I will be able to put myself in the position I need to be in to succeed right from the start. It will cause me to be alert, yet it won't crush me. It will simply shift my strategy, get me out of my comfort zone and teach me something new. The great thing about facing new challenges is that you always learn something as a result.

If you're feeling comfortable about things or even starting to lose interest in your business, then it's likely that you need to start giving yourself more of a challenge. Maybe it would be good for you to take on a new source of business, start working on a new lead generation strategy, or begin sharing with other agents the things you are great at to help them succeed. There are many ways you can challenge yourself in order to grow and improve.

Perhaps a few personal examples may resonate with you. Two years ago, I was completely bored out of my mind with selling real estate. I could sell it in my sleep. There was a series of four different houses that I listed in the months of January and February. All of them had previously been on the market with different agents for over 400 days and failed to sell. I saw this as a fun challenge. I listed them, I followed my proven process, and I sold them all in under 30 days—no problem.

If there's one thing I know for sure about myself, it's that I am driven by challenge. If there's no challenge to something, it makes me lose interest, drive, and motivation. When this happened, I said to myself, "This isn't challenging me anymore." I lost the spark inside. I had to figure out a new way to challenge myself in order to keep my interest, creativity and motivation flowing.

That's when I decided to create an online course to teach other agents how to do what I was doing so easily. I already had a proven process that had repeatable results, and I had been using it for years. The new challenge for me in this adventure was learning all the technology and things I needed to know in order create, package, sell and maintain an online course with the kind of content, tools and systems that produced amazing results.

To accomplish this, I had to change my focus. I had to take my time, effort and money away from actually selling real estate for a while, so I could get the training course off the ground. It was actually quite uncomfortable for me to do this. To other people, what I was doing might not have made any sense. There was no guarantee that the course I decided to pour myself into for months was going to succeed, make money and be worth the effort.

I didn't know for sure that teaching would be right for me, whereas listing and selling real estate had become second nature. I moved forward anyway because I knew the challenge of doing something new would be its own reward, and I knew this challenge would spark some creativity inside me and likely lead me to connections and experiences I would grow from.

I also came up against the same feelings of discomfort when I decided to write this book. Writing a book is scary for most people. It's a huge, daunting task. As I was getting together my ideas and content for this book, I was collaborating with my friend, Anne, and I didn't think I had all the pieces yet for a complete book. I decided, however, that I was going to go for it and get started anyway, because the idea in my head that I wasn't ready was only a limiting belief.

My friend, Anne, having heard me preach almost daily about limiting beliefs and taking imperfect action for a long time, gave it right back to me, thankfully, and she said, "Amy, it's going to be a work in progress. All you really have to do is let it happen and get started."

The truth is, my fear about creating this book was discomfort about doing something new, different and out of my comfort zone. With the knowledge that tackling challenges and accomplishing new things is a big part of what gives me my spark and allows me to thrive, I was able to focus and view the process of writing this book as a reward in itself, a creative journey and challenge.

Get uncomfortable, take risks, keep pushing the envelope on what your vision is for yourself, your business and your life, and create the kind of business and life that you see in your vision.

✓ When you fear failure, ask yourself, "What's the worst that can happen?"

✓ Think about a situation or opportunities that make you uncomfortable. Your awareness around this can highlight your opportunities to grow.

✓ Think about a time when you pushed yourself out of your comfort zone; did it lead to something better?

✓ When you have a vision of what success looks like on the other side of comfort, you can get there faster and push through with greater conviction.

If you aren't getting uncomfortable, you aren't growing.

Chapter 6

Implement Now, Perfect Later

I used to be a perfectionist, then I realized that being perfect caused slow progress towards my goals. One day, I discovered my favorite mantra, "Implement now, perfect later." When I first heard this, it was one of those light-bulb moments for me, and I haven't looked back since.

A couple of years ago, after I had kids, I realized it's not possible to do everything perfectly. That's when I first discovered the quote I shared with you. It resonated with me so deeply that it became my life mantra.

If you talk to anyone that knows me, they'll tell you I've beat them over the head with this phrase. I've realized that I'm not the only one who has perfectionist tendencies. The problem is most people don't even realize it's their desire to do things perfectly that is truly holding them back.

I recognized this immediately after I started teaching others what I know about real estate and giving them tools and systems to use to create the same success for themselves. I noticed that the people weren't yet seeing the results they wanted from my courses and teachings were people who thought they needed to tweak and perfect everything and "make it theirs" before even starting to implement one action.

I used to be the exact same way. When I was given a tool or strategy, my first instinct was to say, "Okay, now I need to make this work for me. I need to modify it, and I need to tweak things until they're perfect."

I began to realize over time that when I had this attitude, a year would slip by, and I'd still NOT have implemented anything new because I was still working on lining everything up and getting everything into the right position before taking action. As a result, time passed me by while I focused on the small details and forgot the big picture. The other challenge with tweaking a new process is that we all have a tendency to conform it to our level of comfort, and that prevents change and growth from happening.

This is why imperfect action is the best action you can take. Now that I have learned this, I look at everything from the perspective of results, and I grade those results on a scale from 1 to 100. If you take imperfect action, and things don't work out perfect, then you're really at 40 out of 100 on the results scale. Imperfect action gets you moving forward, i.e. a 40, whereas perfect action, in theory only, still has you at a 0, no movement forward.

If you take years learning strategies, accumulating tools and developing systems that you never take action on and implement, then you're still at 0 out of 100 on the results scale—and you've wasted a lot of time and opportunity! Even if things don't work out when you attempt something new, you learn more from having real life experiences than you do from notes you take and shove in a drawer, never to surface or be implemented because they aren't yet perfect.

There are many ways to get into action. Implementing a new tool you discover to improve one of your existing systems. Taking an opposite approach to how you would normally do something. When you take action, the important thing to remember is you're experimenting.

While visiting my husband's aunt and uncle one summer, Denise and Brian, my husband and I were introduced to and became big fans of the Moscow mule. Upon our return, my husband began gathering all the tools and ingredients necessary to make his own Moscow mules. We got several kinds of copper mugs, some tarnished, others didn't.

He scoured the city for the perfect kind of ginger beer with no sugar, so he could drink a Moscow mule while he watched his nutrition. He found the best lime juice and experimented and tested all the different ratios of vodka, lime and ginger beer for weeks. He was motivated to recreate a great Moscow mule that fit into his nutritional guidelines AND tasted great.

After many attempts, many taste tests, with feedback about the amount of lime juice and type of ginger beer, he continued to share his attempts and gain feedback each time, making it better. He had a strong "why" and took action with an attitude of "experimentation" for each version and attempt at the perfect Moscow mule. Even to this day, he will give a new ingredient a shot to see if it makes the result even better than the previous. All in all, this has been a great benefit to anyone we entertain as they help him through is experimentation.

When you take an idea, put it into action and see what happens, that's a full circle process. It's experimentation through trial and error. Each result yields a better, yet imperfect version. There might be 30 different things that could happen when you take one action, yet you can't know the outcome until you take the action.

No one expects an experiment to work the first time you make an attempt. It's expected you'll tweak and change direction a few times before you get it right.

Look at these experiments as your permission to experiment with new things! See what happens and see what you learn. If you love to tinker with things and tweak them, there's a time for that. The tweaking stage comes after the action stage. If you start with the tweaking stage before taking action, you may never get started.

You have to get real feedback from an experiment before you can know what you need to do differently next time. This is the only way to grow and make things better. You can't make a quality thing until you've gone through the trial and error process. For this reason, it's beneficial to view everything as a work in progress. Everything you do should always be evolving.

Another way I often see people putting off taking action is by focusing on things that don't matter. I can't tell you how many times I've talked to a new agent who tells me, "I'm so excited. I can't wait to get started selling homes, but I don't have my business cards yet, and I haven't finalized my logo, so I'm not ready to do business yet."

While it's fine to have business cards and a nice-looking logo, not having small things like this should never inhibit you from doing your primary job as a realtor—meeting people and selling houses! You don't need a business card, logo, website, or fancy CRM system to sell a house!

I didn't have a website for the first five years I was a realtor, and I rarely give out my business card even today. Don't get me wrong, these tools can help you, yet they aren't the foundation of a great business. The foundation of a great business is **relationships** with your customers and partners. Relationships take extra effort and nurturing, leading to a mutual trust and respect. When your clients and friends are able to know you, the authentic, true you, they will connect on a deeper level. In a relationship like this, you become an invaluable friend and connector for life. When you have true, authentic relationships with people, a website or business card isn't a necessity. How do you grow relationships? Create opportunities to spend time with people you would like to be in relationship with. Perhaps a client event of like-minded families or empty nesters. Create a community, and watch your relationships and business grow.

Clarity in all aspects of your business is only possible when you take action. Instead of waiting around for everything to make sense to you before doing anything, do anything, and you will be amazed how much valuable, experiential knowledge you will gain—even if you make a mistake!

← Game Plan →

✓ Make a list of 3 things you want to implement in your life or business.

✓ Pick one thing and take one step each day to get it started, begin taking action and experimenting.

✓ Expect to make mistakes and be ready to learn from them, modify and continue the experimentation.

✓ When you face fear, discomfort and speed bumps, ask yourself, "What's the worst that can happen?"

✓ "When this experiment succeeds, what can this experiment's success do for my business and my family?"

What's the worst that can happen?

Chapter 7

Stay in Your Lane

The great thing about running your own business is you can do what you love and what you are great at (these are often the same thing, unsurprisingly!), and then discard or outsource everything else. This is how you stay focused and accomplish incredible things.

Some might lead you to believe that to succeed in business you have to say "yes" to every opportunity that's presented to you. They might lead you to believe that getting really great results is all about cramming more and more activities onto your calendar. Some might even lead you to believe that in order to get something done right, you have to do it yourself, and that no one else can do it better. Yet, at the highest levels of success are the people who have learned to say "no."

You have probably heard the saying, "Good is the enemy of great." What I interpret this to mean is there are a lot of good opportunities out there that can distract you from pursuing the truly great ones. What I've learned over the years is it is much more beneficial to focus on one great opportunity than to chase after hundreds of good ones. Ever heard of the phrase, "Go small to get big?" It's the idea that you need to fine tune a really basic idea of what you want to be great at, and then put all of your effort into that small idea, and it will get better and bigger.

This concept applies to so many different areas of business. For example, in any business, when you attempt to work with everyone who knocks on your door, in essence, you're performing a disservice to the people who could most use your help, and you ultimately serve no one well. This is why it's important to find your niche, focus in, and stick with it. When you do a little bit of everything, you fail to sharpen the most important skills. "Jack of all trades, Master of NONE."

I discovered this for myself when I first started in real estate and was doing all kinds of different things. As time went on, and I tried a little bit of everything, I got clear on what I didn't enjoy or wasn't good at, and that lead to great clarity for me on what I wanted to be my focus. My niche or focus became helping individuals and families experience success with their real estate goals. Your niche may be something different completely; you won't know until you explore and find what makes you tick. Who knows? You might love selling condos in high-rise buildings. It's important to explore and experiment, and then decide what your passion is, and focus in on that.

For example, I don't enjoy the process of working with real estate investors. I don't like focusing on cashflow, capitalization rates and maximizing income on rentals. It's not my passion. As a real estate agent, I get steady requests to take on investor clients. I know this is not my passion or focus, so I have the clarity and conviction to know that, and I refer them to someone I trust who specializes in working with investors. I've learned that it's never worth it to sacrifice my focus, even if an opportunity looks good. This is because the best long-term business growth strategy is to focus on your strengths and what you enjoy; stay in your lane!

Back in 2009, I read the book *StrengthsFinder 2.0* by Tom Rath. I forgot all about this book and what I learned at that time. Then, in 2016, I found the book in a box in my basement while I was looking for some old CDs. When I cracked open the book again for the first time in seven years, I had a major revelation. I realized that all of the successes and struggles I'd experienced since 2009 were more or less related to my specific strengths and weaknesses.

One of the biggest mistakes I see people make is focusing too much on bettering their weaknesses. Improving a weak spot is a good idea in theory, yet in practice it only provides you with marginal improvement.

For example, if you're not great at math, say you are a 1 out of 10 in math, your focus shouldn't be on sitting down and becoming better at it. You might only improve with a lot of effort to a 4 or 5 out of 10. Instead, you should focus on the things you're good at, the things that give you energy and spark.

Let's say you are a really good writer and you really enjoy writing. You are an 8 out of 10 when it comes to writing. With some effort and a good teacher, you can become a 10 out of 10. This is where focusing on your strengths will get you so much further and create more fulfillment than focusing on improving weaknesses.

The book, *StrengthsFinder 2.0,* discusses how if you put your energies into what you're good at, you will get a lot better at those things. When you improve your strengths, they provide you with more wealth in terms of happiness and fulfillment. In other words, you succeed at a higher level and more rapidly when you focus on doing what you're good at.

When you do this, and you pair up with other people that have strengths that you do not, this creates synergy. Synergy is what happens when people come together to accomplish something much greater than they could accomplish on their own. This is why knowing how to maintain your focus and pair up with the right people can make all the difference. Teaming up with the right people doesn't only ADD to your success; the RIGHT people will MULTIPLY your success!

Years ago, I wanted to hire an assistant. I thought the person I wanted to hire should be a lot like me. I wanted them to be driven, motivated, a self-starter, a people person, and share my interests. Eventually, I realized that I didn't need another one of me. I needed the opposite of me. I needed somebody that was detail oriented, followed instructions, likes order and consistency.

Even in personal relationships, we have counter balanced strengths and weaknesses. For example, a few years ago (not in the 1980s, mind you) I wanted a dust buster to clean up the crumbs from the kids at the table. I mentioned to my husband that I wanted a dust buster, and he began his research. He started looking at Consumer Reports and reviews on Amazon, etc. His strength is investigating and researching options, and he is great at this!

A week later, I asked about the dust buster. He was still researching and hadn't purchased one yet. Later that afternoon, I was at Target, and I decided to buy a dust buster off of the shelf that looked good to me. I brought it home, used it once, and the next day it was broken. Ultimately, I'm not sure who won there, yet as a husband

and wife, we are aware of each of our strengths and work together to create the best outcomes for our family. Understanding this about each other as a married couple, and then understanding this about those we work with as a team, makes a huge impact on our success.

When it comes to putting a winning team together, be honest with yourself, identify strengths you have and find people with strengths that you don't have, so you can identify your counterparts to multiply success.

Stay in your lane with what you enjoy and are great at. Let go of what takes your energy away because clients can see this. Excel at your strengths and more opportunity will follow. Identify others that you will work in great synergy with to cause a multiplication of success.

Game Plan

✓ Get the *Strengths Finder 2.0* book and take the assessment. Read about your top 5 strengths and absorb the information.

✓ Be honest with yourself about what your strengths are.

✓ Look for others to complete your yin/yang.

✓ Keep focused and working in your strengths and watch your success multiply.

✓ BONUS: Get Amy's recommended book list at www.amyb.com/booklist

Multiply your successes and positive energy by focusing on your strengths.

Chapter 8

Is It a "Hell YES"?

I'm a very out-in-the-community type of person. When people see me, they know who I am and what I do. When you sell a lot of real estate, you're known and seen as a leader in your community; you are somebody that gets things done.

My kids started school last year, and this coming year will be our second year in the school system. Recently, I was approached by the PTA and asked to join one of the committees at the school.

When I got this email asking me to join, I let it sit there for a couple of days. I didn't know what to do with it. I felt a lot of "mom guilt" coming on. I couldn't decide what the right thing for me to do was.

I looked at the list of committees I'd been asked to lead several times, and none of the things on the list sparked my passion. Nothing was screaming at me, "Amy, this is an awesome challenge you will have a passion for!"

When I was contemplating how to respond, I talked to a friend of mine about what I should do. She, like me, is a high producing real estate agent whose kids are now in middle school. She shared my guilt, and she was gracious enough to be honest with me and tell me what I needed to know and hear. Her response was, "Amy, can I be honest with you?"

Now, if you've been paying attention, you know that of course I want people to be honest and get to the point! My response was, "Yes, please! I'm struggling with how to respond."

Then, she hit me with it. She said, "You're not PTA material." She wasn't trying to offend me. She went on to say that I was better suited for other things. My connections in the community as a real estate agent put me in a better position to help the school board raise money for a project or purchase a new building or land they might need.

Having my friend tell me this was eye opening to me. Even though I knew already that it's best for me to focus on my passions and things I find challenging, it was still hard for me to say no. And if I had chosen to spend my time doing what was asked of me because I felt like I had to, it would have taken away from the time I have available to do something more meaningful and helpful.

I've learned over time how important it is to constantly take inventory of what you're saying "hell yes" to and what you're saying "no" to. When you choose to do something, you have to recognize this means you're saying "no" to something else. You might be saying "no" to your business partner or even your kids and your spouse when you choose to say "yes" to something. The decisions you make, however small or large, ultimately decide the direction your life is going to take. My friend and mentor Hank always says, "With each step you take, you are either moving yourself towards or away from your goals."

When faced with a decision, you have to ask yourself if what you're considering doing is going to inch you forward towards your goals or not. If the answer isn't a "Hell YES," then it should be an automatic "no."

Not to say that remaining focused is a cakewalk. I'll be the first one to tell you that I'm often like a squirrel in the middle of the road going in a million different directions. Just the other day I came home from a meeting with an idea a partner of mine suggested in my head, to do a seminar on downsizing for older home owners.

Thankfully, my husband listened to me and asked, "How does that fit in with your goals and priorities?" He reminded me that my focus is on families, not those downsizing right now, and that even though the seminar was a good idea, it didn't truly align with my focus. The good idea would take away from the great goals, plans and visions I had set; it would not add to them. In the big picture, it was a "good" idea, yet not a "great" one that fit my master plan. (Remember, good is the enemy of great.)

This is why it's great to share your goals and visions with the people around you, your cheerleaders. They can keep you accountable in times like these. Another way to keep yourself accountable is to pay attention to what things excite you. While this has the potential to lead you off course sometimes, once you know who you are and what you're good at, excitement is a great indicator for what you should be learning about, researching and focusing on.

To put it simply, if you're not excited to get up and go to work, then you're probably doing the wrong thing. If you have no passion for what you're doing, then you're doing the world and most importantly yourself, a disservice by doing something you don't enjoy. Find your passion and vision, go all in, and watch it multiply.

This reminds me of a recent lunch meeting I had with a woman who started in real estate around the same time I did. She recently left the business. At lunch, I asked her, "Why did you get out of real estate? You were doing great."

She told me, "I didn't like that my life was working all the time, and I felt unappreciated by my clients. It wasn't worth the money anymore. I wanted to be happy." It made me sad that she didn't have access to the tools and concepts that could have corrected this for her and allowed her to stay in the thriving business she had built for herself over 10+ years. These issues are typical obstacles for a lot of people in the real estate business, and they can be overcome and corrected when you create the proper standards and boundaries to protect yourself from falling prey to them.

As a real estate agent, sometimes you must take charge and set the right parameters for your business. I'm able to effectively work with my clients Monday through Friday between 7:30 a.m. and 4:30 p.m. I didn't have to quit real estate to accomplish this, yet I did have to be willing to say "no" to clients. At first, "no" was uncomfortable—then I saw the multiplication of happiness in my business, finances and life that resulted, and I can't imagine life any other way.

If I had never learned to say "no," then my personal life and my career would not be sustainable. If you're an agent, and you had no idea you were allowed to say "no" to meetings and phone calls outside of the hours you've set for yourself, I hope reading this sets you free.

← Game Plan →

✓ What are you saying "yes" to that isn't your passion?

✓ Keep a "good" list on the wall. Use it to remember good ideas that don't make the "great" list this year. Realize they may or may not make the "great" list for next year.

✓ Ask yourself, "If I say 'YES' to this, what am I

Focus is about saying NO.

Steve Jobs

Chapter 9

Letting Go and Saying NO

The first several years of my real estate career, I was a solo agent working with buyers and sellers. I was doing all kinds of business. I was listing, buying, and on top of that I was newly married.

My husband loved to golf. Golf was his game, and real estate was my game. I enjoyed it, and I felt very fortunate to be doing work that I enjoyed. I was always focused on improving, and I still am. There are all kinds of metrics you can change in the game of real estate in order to improve your net or results. I've gotten very good at the game, yet I still face obstacles. They're now simply different than they were in the beginning.

I didn't start growing my team until I hit a wall selling more homes than I ever had in a year by the month of July, all on my own. At this point, I finally said, "This isn't fun anymore. This is too much."

Our friends were getting married over the 4th of July weekend, so we went out of town for the 4th of July weekend, and I completely broke down. I realized I couldn't keep up the pace I was going at. I had to reinvent my business and leverage what I was doing in a different way. I didn't know how I was going to do that, yet I knew something had to change.

Because I needed to relax, recover and clear my head, we decided to extend our trip. We turned our short trip into a longer vacation because I desperately needed a break long enough to gain perspective and create a game plan that would create the work/life balance that I needed to endure in this business.

I happened to have Gary Keller's book, *Shift*, with me. I hadn't read it yet. After a couple of days, I was lying out by the pool and decided to crack it open. As soon as I started reading, I started to identify with a lot of the ideas in the book, and I realized I had been working on recreating the wheel in my business.

I saw that there were already people who had done the same things as me, faced the same challenges, and figured out how to overcome them. Inspired by what I learned, I decided to make a shift in my own business by becoming a listing specialist and hiring a buyer's agent to handle all my buyer transactions.

A buyer's agent is somebody who specializes in working with our clients that are buying homes, only making purchases. Having a buyer's agent on my team I realized would free me up to focus only on listings. Not only would this give me back massive amounts of time, it would also mean that when someone came to work with me, they would get two specialist realtors to take care of both their need to sell and their need to buy.

Before I had a buyer's agent on my team, there were days when I would actually hesitate to put a new listing on the market because I knew it would sell immediately. Then I'd have to have those now homeless sellers in the car with me the next whole day looking for houses. It was like a marathon to get a listing on the market, negotiate it, and then immediately start looking for another home and begin negotiating that purchase, too.

It was too much for only one person to do, especially in a busy or difficult market. It made sense to break this into two jobs. When I finally made this change in my business, it made my life more predictable and more tolerable. It allowed me to focus on my business and guide clients through my processes on my schedule. It enabled me to achieve greater balance, be happier, and have a better life.

The biggest thing I had to learn in order to bring my life back into balance was how to release control. Real estate agents and entrepreneurs in general tend to be self-starters, and as a consequence they also tend to think they are the best person to do every single job that needs to be done in their business. To be fair, this is because in the beginning we often do all the jobs. And if you attempt to do everything in your business on your own, you will always end up burning yourself out, and that will show to clients before long.

Giving up control or "letting go" and creating balance in your life and business requires a mindset shift. It's not about pulling yourself up by your bootstraps. It's about letting go of the bootstraps, finding someone who is better than you at some aspect of your business, and then trusting them to do it.

You don't lose anything when you do this because it means you can focus on doing what you're best at. When everyone who is a part of your team is doing what they're good at, everyone can have an amazing experience. Letting go is yet another example of multiplication vs. addition in your life.

Working in real estate is an experience like no other. For the most part, it means a constant barrage of phone calls, text messages and negotiations that don't go away on holidays or when you're on vacation. Most people expect you to always be working, and this can be exhausting. There are still times when I turn everything off and get away for a while. There are times when you MUST say NO. Humans need recovery time away from work to revitalize and return creativity. Problem solvers like real estate agents need recovery time more than most. Ironically, this recovery time is the thing we and our clients almost never allow ourselves to have. And it's this recovery time that gives us the spark to solve the problems and negotiations for our clients and business.

As I've mentioned, every evening I make sure I'm home by 4:30 p.m. because that's when my husband and I have agreed we will be together for family time (exception being today, while he is graciously in a quiet place editing this book to meet our publisher's deadline). The agreement we made with each other is that we will both be there to make a healthy dinner with our family, and then we will spend the evening together. Our kids go to bed at 8 p.m. So from 4:30 to 8 is not a lot of time to spend with the people who are most important to you in your life. That's why we protect this time for our family to make sure it's quality time.

If I must negotiate a contract during these family, quality time hours, I tell the client, "We can talk at 8 o'clock tonight, or we can wait until 8 a.m. tomorrow morning when I'm in the office with my files and everything in place to get this thing done." I simply give people alternative options. I feel no need to justify why I'm not available around the clock.

If someone can't work with me within the hours that I make myself available, then I might suggest another agent that can better meet their expectations. I don't like to do this, yet it happens. If you give somebody an inch, they'll take a mile. Setting expectations early on and honoring them helps maintain the balance for your well-being and for your family.

If I need to work on a weekend, it's only to negotiate a contract. Beyond that, I am not available. Everything that needs to be done can be done during the week and during business hours. You can create this balance in your business as well. No one else is going to do it for you. It's going to be uncomfortable at first, and you'll need to experiment with how to do it successfully. Yet if you can have conviction for the kind of business and life you want, you will find a way to say "no."

- ✓ What can you let go in order for someone else to do it better and you get more time back?

- ✓ What are your least favorite tasks at home/work? Hire those out to get better results and keep your energy and focus on your strengths.

- ✓ Do you have a written "ideal" schedule?

- ✓ Do you have a focused work place that allows you to be efficient with your time?

"You have to decide
what your highest priorities are
and have the courage —
pleasantly, smiling,
nonapologetically — to say no to
other things.
And the way to do that is by
having a bigger 'yes' burning
inside."

Stephen Covey

Chapter 10

The Real Estate Rollercoaster

When you first begin as a real estate agent, it's always a struggle because as you make money, you're suddenly responsible for allocating it for taxes, licensing fees, marketing, technology and many other things. The more money you make, the more all of these things cost. It's simply a part of the business.

To be extremely transparent, my very first full year in real estate in 2006 was a great year for me. I didn't realize what my tax bill for the year was going to be. When it came time to do taxes, I ended up owing the IRS $25,000 that I didn't have. It took me until June of the following year to pay this money back.

There are worse things that could have happened to me in my first year, yet this was eye opening and a huge learning moment. I said to myself, "I will never, ever let this happen again. Never." I knew I needed to get help making sure my finances were in order from that point on, so my husband and I decided to hire a professional to help us. More on that decision to come.

Next, I had a formidable learning experience while working with a guy who wanted to buy a house. He was looking for a home in the $400,000 range, and it was November. I didn't have anything else on the books, Christmas was coming up, and I felt obligated to make sure this guy bought a house as soon as possible because we needed the money.

The problem was the guy was a complete slime ball. He always had me meet him at the bar he was drinking at around 6 p.m., wait for him to finish his drink, and then he would go look at one house—always only one. Let's just say I don't think he would have invited a male real estate agent to meet him in this manner.

Regardless of his reasons, I didn't like the way I felt having to do this all the time. I felt like he was taking advantage of me, and I thought what he was doing was totally inappropriate. The reality was I needed the money— so I continued to pick him up at the bar to see homes until he finally bought one.

Finally, he found a house, and I was able to sell it to him. Once the transaction was complete, I told myself that from that day on I would never put myself in that position again. I knew from that moment on that I had to earn a living on my terms, so I could CHOOSE to eliminate situations like this from my life.

Fast forward to the solution for this rollercoaster of real estate income. My husband and I got married in 2006, and we didn't know how to "merge" or combine our incomes and bills and create a budget together. On top of that challenge, while my husband had a consistent salary income, I on the other hand had a very inconsistent income, which I call "The Real Estate Rollercoaster." One month I would make a ton of money, and the next month I'd make none. This made it very hard to create our budget. We needed the help of a professional that had succeeded with a challenge like this before.

Next, we sat down with our financial and budget professional, Jason, and he helped us figure out a budget for the money we had. Every month we stuck to it, and we each had the same amount to spend whether I made $20,000 that month or zero dollars. The most important thing we did after working with Jason was start putting money into a reserve account for those months when no money would come in.

When you have money put aside in reserve, you don't have to feel stressed and desperate if you have a slow month because that reserve money is there to kick in to cover expenses. We decided to put six months of reserve money aside to help us weather a storm or a slower month, because slow months are a reality in real estate. Now, we had a game plan for that rollercoaster.

We worked hard to get our finances in order, so I could be in control and choose to work with clients that were respectful, appropriate and that I enjoyed. Making the decision to start setting cash reserves aside is one of the best decisions I've ever made as a realtor. Already having money in the bank gives you the confidence needed to make better choices for yourself about what clients you're willing take on.

This concept doesn't only apply to avoiding working with jerk clients. It also plays a role in day to day real estate agent situations. For example, if someone comes to me and wants to list their house for $250,000, and I believe it's only going to bring $200,000 on the market, I'm not afraid to tell them that. I can walk away from a conversation or opportunity like that confidently because I've already got money in the bank. Saying "no" feels right sometimes. With a funded reserve, you can know you will be fine.

All you have to do to get this power is follow a budget and set aside your extra cash in your reserve. Don't take that $10,000 closing check and spend it in one month simply because you have it. You don't know when the next deal will come through, so you need a game plan.

Real estate agents tend to be enticed by shiny objects because we're paid in big lump sums, and it's tempting to unload them quickly. The 100 people a day that solicit real estate agents know this, too... That's why they call us, relentlessly. I can't tell you how many phone calls I get from people who want to sell me something—leads, websites, marketing. There's only one thing I can say to these salesmen that gets them to hang up the phone

When you respond with, "That's not in my budget," they know you're at a level where you're serious about your business, and they're not going to waste their time trying to convince you to buy something you don't need. If you use the word budget, they'll know you're financially literate (maybe even a little sophisticated) and not susceptible to their sales tactics.

Do any of these apply to you today?

- You're just getting started in real estate
- You don't have a budget in place
- You've never made a variable income before
- You aren't used to paying your own expenses
- You've never had to pay quarterly taxes

If so, then you need to figure this out ASAP because living on a variable income is different than living on a predictable one. Not everyone can figure out how to do this on their own. Even the top producing agents in the country hire professionals to do their taxes, and they know the importance of investing in expert guidance to make sure their financial future and security stays strong.

If you're part of a husband and wife team, some of the biggest challenges you will face together will be in regard to finances. Having a third party come in and direct you on how you to set up your finances takes the weight off of any one of you.

I'm not a financial advisor myself and because everyone's business varies drastically, I'm not going to give you percentages for how you should structure your budget. As it relates to doing business as a real estate agent, the one thing I can tell you is that you want to have six months of reserves in the bank. This is because if you're a brand-new agent, you can expect to go 60 to 90 days before you complete your first sales cycle. If you expect to get results faster than this, you're kidding yourself. Even if you're a seasoned vet, you know that a rough market can stall your income and getting back on track can take 30+ days due to escrow closing times.

It's better to have a cash reserve when you first jump into real estate than to take a side job. No matter what kind of business you're in, a side job it will only take your time and focus away from what you should be focused on. Instead of distracting yourself with work you don't want to be doing, save money in your reserve first, and then go all-in on your business.

The best thing I ever did for my business, and the one thing I always recommend every real estate agent do is get someone to help you with a budget and help you get your reserves in order. Until you do this, you're going to be riding the real estate rollercoaster.

← Game Plan →

✓ Hire a financial advisor to guide you in budgeting, reserves and tax liability the day you start selling real estate.

✓ Save 6 months of reserves (monthly expenses) ideally before you start or ASAP and keep 6 months always.

✓ Say no to slime balls.

"Mo money,

Mo Problems."

The Notorious B.I.G.

Chapter 11

Let it GO!

I used to think I was a big quitter. I thought I gave up on things too easily. Sometimes it would seem to others that I didn't work at something hard enough, or that I should keep attempting to do something for a longer period of time. After reading *StrengthsFinder 2.0*, I discovered this is a strength of mine. Who knew that being a quitter could be turned into a strength!

I've somehow always had an intuitive grasp of the concept of sunk cost bias, I never knew the term before reading the book *Essentialism* by Greg McKeown. Sunk cost bias is the idea that if you attempt to do something and it doesn't succeed after a good attempt and a fair amount of time, then you need to cut your losses and move on. Conversely, the typical thought process is that, with enough persistence and hard work, anything is possible. While I'm not disputing that idea, there has to be a limitation to how much you will invest before the labor of the effort will never result in an outcome that is as valuable as if you would simply move your efforts on to something else. A lot of people have great challenges with this concept; in the end, it's always been how I operate.

One great example of sunk cost bias occurs frequently in romantic relationships. People often get into a relationship, and after a certain amount of time, they know it's not going well. Instead of ending things right then, they say to themselves, "I can't leave this relationship. I've already invested so much time and energy into it!" Ironically, the more time they invest into it, the harder it becomes for them to walk away. They are also missing opportunities to find a better romantic relationship because they are distracted with this person that they know deep down isn't the right person for them.

The way I view things, if someone or something is not right for you, you need to cut things off as soon as you know. This concept is so important when it comes to selling real estate. Sometimes as an agent you will put so much time, effort and energy into selling a specific home, and things will string along for months on end. Often the house isn't priced right, or it isn't in the right condition and doesn't sell.

After a certain point, you have to be able to say to your client, "Hey, this isn't working. I've tried everything I can to sell your house, and I need to move on." This is something that comes naturally to me. I cut my losses quicker than most because I know when it's time to move on to something else that makes me excited or is a better investment of my time or money.

There are so many times as agents that we take a listing, and we keep it forever because we've already invested time and money in it. We keep it even when we know it's not going to sell because the client isn't motivated, and the price isn't right.

At some point, you have to take the time, effort and energy you're spending on things that are getting you nowhere and put it into something else that will get somewhere. That might mean putting it into a new client who is prepared to do what it takes to get their home sold. The same principal applies to working with buyers.

I feel so bad for agents when they tell me they've shown people 100 plus homes. When this is the case, something is clearly not working. You're not meeting their expectations somehow; perhaps they don't know what they want, it doesn't exist, they don't have enough money, or you aren't understanding their needs. Either way, it's time to part ways. They should find another agent. You should find new clients.

Some agents will say, "I've spent five tanks of gas driving these people around. I've spent days doing this when I should have been at the soccer field with my kids. They're going to buy a $400,000 house eventually, so I have to stick with it, or all of this will have been for nothing."

Until I learned about sunk cost bias, I always had this inner belief that I was a quitter when I walked away in situations like this. Now I have enough experience to know I need to be listening to myself when there's a voice in my head screaming, "Enough is enough! I've given this a fair shake and it's not working."

Many agents are afraid that walking away means they are letting their client down, yet that's not necessarily true. Most of the time if things aren't progressing, clients and agents are relieved when ways are parted. Generally, you're both frustrated and need a break.

As a last-ditch effort to squeeze one last drop out of a situation like this, you can share with the client that you don't believe you can meet their expectations. This may cause them to ask if they are being unrealistic, giving you permission to be honest. If you say "YES," they will either adjust their expectations and buy a house, or they will go find another agent that will attempt to meet their unrealistic expectations for another 100 showings and 5 more tanks of gas. Either way, you win!

Game Plan

✓ Be honest with yourself, what do you need to quit today?

✓ How can you release a client and still feel good about it later?

✓ Do you recall a time when you fired a client? How did you feel after?

✓ What does your ideal client look like to you? What are your standards for your ideal client? What expectations do you have of them?

Cutting your losses is one of the BEST decisions NEVER made.

Chapter 12

Build Your Tribe

Be careful who you take advice from because you'll turn into them. Whatever kind of bait you put on your hook is the kind of fish you're going to catch. Think about that before you put something out there.

I see people on Facebook all the time who go into real estate groups and ask questions like, "What's the best way to generate leads? What CRM should I use?" The list goes on and on for advice people seek in these groups.

Let's slow down and think here for a moment. Does it even make sense to be asking these questions in a random group where some random person you don't even know is going to answer? Crowdsourcing fairly critical business information in a sea of people. Yikes.

In my opinion, this doesn't make sense at all. You don't even know for sure if the person who is responding to you is actually in business for themselves, or if they're responding to your post in order to sell you a product. You have to vet people before you ask them for their advice.

The best thing you can do when you are new or are looking for advice on growth or teambuilding, etc., is to seek out a tribe of people that walk the walk and talk the talk—that have the results and the successes that you want to have. Then do all you can to mimic and learn from them.

Everyone is always looking for the magic potion. They're looking for the silver bullet. In this day and age, everybody thinks that technology is going to save them from doing everything they don't want to do. Sometimes technology can help with a certain aspect of business, and sometimes it can't. Be wary of the people who insist you can only succeed with the latest technology. Technology is there to make your work more efficient and to give your clients a better experience. If that isn't what the technology in question is doing, I'd think again about your reasons for considering it.

Instead, look for the people out there, myself included, who will give you the game plan for success and encourage you to get out there and fight to win. You have to do the work. You have to implement what you learn. You have to make it happen. No amount of technology is going to automate you out of your business. You will always have to add value to the process as a human being. And that's a damn good thing, too!

When you're investigating the best way to get started in real estate, many will tell you that you should join a team. Very few teams are created and set up on a foundation that will survive and even thrive. It's not any easier to be on or create a team as it is to be a solo agent. I've done both and I've seen both in action.

If somebody is encouraging you to be on a team, take their advice with a grain of salt, and talk to some people who were on that team and left it, and talk to some who are still a part of the team. Do your due diligence, and explore your options intelligently, carefully and thoroughly. Take your time.

If you need advice for how to get started in real estate, ask people who have succeeded in the industry for a long period of time. Don't only go talk to people who are one year ahead of you. Ask people who are four or ten years ahead of you. Get them to tell you how they started in the beginning and where they are at today. There are too many people selling formulas for success that they haven't even proven to be true for themselves.

Show gratitude for those that take the time to invest in YOU and raise you up. Simone Weil, a French philosopher, said, "Attention is the rarest and purest form of generosity." What I take this to mean is that appreciating others and showing gratitude to people who take the time to help, encourage, train and teach you is important.

Everybody is so busy, yet taking the time to make someone else better in some way, to lift them up or give them the tools they need, is so important. It's also important to express your thanks when someone gives you their time. One of the best ways you can thank them is to really listen to what they have to share with you by giving them your full attention.

In fact, giving proper attention to all areas of your life is very important, and it's something many people neglect to do. For me, giving my full attention to my children is a huge priority because I recognize the fact that I only have one chance to build a relationship with them as they grow up, and I know how valuable that relationship is.

What you focus on is what will expand in your life. We are all wired in different ways. I'm an achiever, so I'm naturally always ready to get started on the next project. One thing I have to watch out for is not taking the time to really appreciate what I've accomplished and celebrate it. Most people in business for themselves don't give themselves enough credit for their accomplishments.

If selling three houses in a month is a big deal to you, give yourself a damn pat on the back for doing that because no one else is going to do it for you. Appreciate yourself and give yourself attention, too! When you take time to feel good about an accomplishment, you're giving yourself an incentive to go out and do it again.

Allow yourself to celebrate your successes and give yourself some grace when you don't succeed, so you can look forward to when you do. As Oprah says, "The more you praise and celebrate life, the more there is in life to celebrate."

There's a great interview of Steve Harvey with Oprah where he says, "If you're always complaining about your situation, God's not going to give you the good stuff. If you're thankful for all the good stuff that you have, he'll give you more good stuff."

Placing your attention on the positive things that are happening in your life will shape your mindset for success. This is how you put yourself in a position to receive more good into your life.

You have to start by being thankful for what you have, and then get ready to grow. If you're in a pile of mud, be grateful that the pile of mud you're in is close to a hose so you can clean yourself off. There's always a silver lining to any situation if you place your attention on finding it. The faster you build yourself up out of the mud with even the smallest of wins, the more momentum you will build up on your side to carry you through to the next great part of your journey.

If you want to pay a premium price for a pep talk with no real substance, learning from someone that can't prove their success or results might mean that's what you'll end up getting. If you're serious about your business, only take advice from people who know what they're talking about and can prove it. Then, surround yourself with a like-minded tribe of people you desire to be like.

← Game Plan →

✓ Identify 3-5 people that you admire based on their business success. Seek them out and absorb any of their suggestions and content to get as much from them as you can.

✓ Identify 3-5 people that you admire as a human being. Seek them out and learn from their lessons.

✓ Who do you know that has similar goals as you do? How can you help each other reach your individual goals? Seek out and bring these like-minded people into your circle or tribe.

"Surround yourself with people who add value to your life. Who challenge you to be greater than you were yesterday. Who sprinkle magic into your existence, just like you do into theirs. Life isn't meant to be done alone. Find your tribe, and journey freely and loyally together."

Alex Elle

Chapter 13

Rebounding from a Bad Situation

Real estate deals with high emotion and high dollars. When we talk about homes, we're talking about places where people live, eat, sleep and raise their families. A home is where you raise your children and where life's most important events occur.

For most people, when they buy a home, it's the most money they've ever spent on a single transaction in their lives. They spend so many sleepless nights getting ready to make this purchase, and it's not only the purchase that's stressful. Many emotions tend to come up when people are packing up and moving into a new place.

Hurt feelings come into play. Couples can't agree on what color to paint a wall. They don't like the way a yard looks. Big emotions can surface about little things, and sometimes they can all come crashing down on your head as the realtor who is responsible for making sure every 'I' has been dotted and 'T' has been crossed.

When clients are dealing with intense emotions and a large financial investment, the job of the real estate agent is to stay objective and business focused. It can be a challenge for an agent not to become too emotional themselves.

As an agent, you may have to stay up late at night putting things in order. You may have to work a lot of hours in a short period of time. Combine all of this with working with people who you start to care for and really want to help, and it can be easy to let your emotions get the best of you. Yet you can't let that happen. You have to always remain professional and keep a business focus.

It gets crazy, and unless you've been an agent for some time, you may not understand all of the emotional parts of it yet. Trust me when I say that there will come a time when you will have to maintain your composure while everyone around you is going nuts. Sometimes all you can do is barely move the needle in the right direction, you have to keep things moving forward at whatever pace is manageable.

This is why I believe there will always be real estate agents involved with home buying transactions because the job simply can't be done by a computer. There are too many human factors involved in it. I always let my clients know from the start that the whole process is going to be emotional, and that my job is to stay objective and keep things moving forward. This helps set the expectation for how we will work together throughout the whole process.

No matter how tight of a ship you run, if you work in real estate for any length of time, you will run into people who are simply unfair to you. Many people simply don't understand all the things their real estate agent is doing to help them. This makes it easy to start to feel unappreciated and taken for granted.

One of my mentors, Jamie, told me early on that, "If you're not meeting your fair share of crazy people, you're not doing enough business."

You're going to get hit. You're going to get knocked down, and you have to be able to pick yourself up and keep moving forward. Learning how to recover from that is what's important. To quote one of the best boxing movies of all time, "It ain't about how hard you hit. It's about how hard you can get hit and keep moving forward." To keep moving forward, you have to focus on your own attitude, because ultimately that's the only thing you have complete control over.

All of those external feelings and words being thrown around are sending a message. Sometimes it doesn't make sense. If you can control your internal reaction to the noise, you can learn something about the situation.

A couple of weeks ago, I had a really awful closing. The night before the closing was supposed to happen, my clients put all the stuff they didn't want from their house out at the curb—couches, paintings, etc. Their stuff spanned from one end of the property to the other. The buyers' agent called me, as I hadn't seen this pile, and we identified where the contract states "trash or treasure, remove your belongings before closing."

I was the one who had to tell my clients they had to remove this stuff before the closing; they couldn't leave it for the garbage service that wouldn't come until a few days after the closing. They were not happy. I know they hadn't slept well, probably on an air mattress, and were short on nerves with packing and moving. So, the next morning on my way to the closing, I decided to go to my favorite donut store, Marcella's, and get a dozen donuts to bring to the closing as a way to create some good and fun energy.

At the table that morning, these people didn't even want to make eye contact with me. They only talked to me about what was necessary to move the closing forward. I was the messenger, and they did not like the message I delivered. They told me directly, "We don't want your donuts."

When I left the closing, it was nine in the morning, and I seriously contemplated eating all of the donuts myself. I was upset because I had done a great job for them after a previous attempt at selling with another agent had failed. They got a great price, great terms and everything had gone wonderfully until this last minute, ungodly amount of inappropriate trash on the lawn issue.

I had to change my energy at 9 a.m. so the rest of my day didn't follow suit. I had other clients and colleagues depending on me to have great energy and to work hard for them. There was no way to change what had happened at that closing.

I've learned that when I get upset, I need to get into gratitude. So, I thought to myself, "Who can I give these donuts to that deserves them and will appreciate them?"

I decided I should deliver them to the fire department. I'd been there before with my kids, and they had let them explore the trucks and ask questions, so I thought this would be a nice way to say thank you to them. I knew the back door was where they all hung out, so I knocked on the door, and two firemen came out.

I told them, "I've got a donut emergency. Can you help me? I got these donuts for somebody, and they didn't want them, so I thought I should bring them to you guys to thank you for keeping us safe."

They happily took the donuts, and from there I went to my office. I quickly hopped on a focused conference call for about an hour. The minute I got off the conference call, my phone was blowing up. It was my husband, so I answered, and he told me, "Don't freak out. Everything is okay, our house caught on fire a little bit, it's out now. Can you come home?"

My office is two miles from our house, so I went home. When I got home there was no smoke, no fire, no nothing. The fire department was there winding up the hoses they must have just used to put out the fire. And wouldn't you know? The same two guys I gave the donuts to not more than two hours ago were right there standing in my front yard. I couldn't believe it. They even said to me, "How'd you know we would be visiting your house today when you dropped off those donuts?" (If you're curious, it was just a small mulch fire with a LOT of smoke.)

Recently, I decided to surprise the teachers, staff and bus drivers at my son's school with donuts as a way of saying thank you before the school year came to a close. When I ordered the donuts, Carmen from Marcella's called to verify that I had meant to order 10 dozen.

When I told her why I had ordered so many, she said, "A donut is a great way to make a person's day and bring them joy." Then I told her the donut story I just shared with you, she told me it was the best donut story she'd ever heard.

The point I'm working on making with all this talk of donuts is that getting into gratitude and appreciating other people is a great way to recover from a bad situation. That's the message I choose to see when being delivered bad emotions. Depending on the circumstance, you might learn something about someone or a situation—but only if you're able to separate your reaction to the noise.

People ask me all the time what to do in these situations to cope because these difficult situations and issues are totally normal things for an agent to experience regularly. My best advice is to get into gratitude and stop thinking about yourself so much.

I've done things like buying a meal for someone, writing notes of gratitude to people in your life, dropping donuts off somewhere for other people to enjoy, or simply giving someone an unexpected compliment. There are so many different ways you can show gratitude, and when you do, you will automatically distract yourself from negativity by default. Gratitude and negativity can't share space in your mind at the same time. It's simply not possible.

When you do positive, nice things for other people, you can feel that energy coming back to you. You don't have to stay in negativity and let it carry you away. You can choose to feel better by brightening someone else's day however you see fit.

Game Plan

✓ Next time you have anxiety or stress around a situation, get into gratitude.
- Buy donuts
- Get some fun note cards
- Send some video thank you messages

✓ Stress is a reality in this business. Be prepared to address this kind of stress with:
- Exercise
- Walks
- Meditation

Interrupt

Anxiety

with

Gratitude.

Chapter 14

Win Your Net Life

My business is by referral only, and I recently had a conversation with another agent who shared with me that she was jealous of my referral-based clients. My response was, "I'm glad! That means you are discovering that you prefer relationship-based business over transactional business. Referrals are the best kind of business to have."

It's very fulfilling to work for clients who appreciate you, trust you, and like you. When you do a great job for someone, and they refer you to their friends and family, it's the greatest honor you could receive. The referral of another client should be the goal of each and every sale.

A referral-based business can only happen when you treat people the way you want to be treated. If you want to make a quick buck, it doesn't work. If you are focused on hurrying up, getting your sign in the yard and closing on a contract, you're going to be transactional, a one and done kind of agent.

My clients are my "real estate family." I don't care if you bought a house with me nine years ago or two days ago, I help everyone who has ever been a client of mine do what's best for each of them and their families. This could mean helping someone decide to move now or wait a few years, to helping someone decide if adding additional space to their home is worth the investment.

I do my best to stay in relationship with people. I enjoy my real estate family and create fun events to keep in touch with them throughout the year, be it an ice cream social or photos with Santa. I'm very intentional about this area of my business, and I truly enjoy the relationships that I've created with my clients and their families.

My clients are my friends. There's no gray area here. If you're a client, you're a friend, and if you're a friend, you're at least a potential client. The key to making this work is having integrity, being authentic and honest, and doing your job the best way you know how every single time.

Creating a referral only business will only work if you give people a great experience. They need to have the kind of experience that they feel compelled to tell other people about. This isn't always easy, yet it's the most rewarding kind of business and relationships you can have. When your work is rewarding, you are passionate about it—that will show and your clients will continue to share their great experiences with everyone they know.

The key to making sure your clients have a great experience is to have a system or methodology you follow with everyone. This means everyone gets treated with the best service and care, and everyone is able to build a trusting connection with you. Invest in each and every person who chooses to work with you, with the expectation that doing the best you can for them will give you the opportunity to help even more people down the road. I find my success in rewarding relationships that lead to a business with high integrity. How about you?

What is NET LIFE to you? What are the things in your life and business that are most important to you? What are the things in your life that you are most grateful for? When was the last time you took the time to reflect on what is important to you in your business and life? Until you take the time to identify what is important to you, you cannot create your best life, or your NET LIFE.

Take some time and focus. Be authentic, be you, and you will attract the kind of people and clients that allow you to have a true passion for your work. When you enjoy your work, and those that you serve, that shines through as success. Success attracts all the best people to you, your business and your life. Keep an open mind and an open heart to receive them and help them experience their own successes.

It is my wish that you find your own heart's meaning of success in business and life, and that you can create your best NET LIFE from the game plans in this book.

Live your best life.

Work to LIVE your best life, your NET LIFE!

Game Plan

- ✓ Make a list of the things you are <u>most</u> <u>grateful for</u> in your life/business.

- ✓ Make a list of the things you are <u>most proud</u> <u>of</u> in your life/business.

- ✓ Look at those two lists and identify 3-5 main themes or topics; these are your Priorities.

- ✓ Identify the most important thing you can do to feed and nurture each of your Priorities each week.

- ✓ This is your NET LIFE plan.

"Do what you do
so well
that they will want to
see it again
and bring their
friends."

Walt Disney

What's NEXT?

Take the next step! Implement the *Playbook for Success* into your own life and share it with others! Visit us at www.amyb.com to learn more.

Online Courses

Amy's online courses offer both self-guided and live video trainings, focused on either listing in **Sell 100% of Your Listings**, or the buyer course, **The Ultimate Buyer Loyalty Process**. Each course comes with professionally designed documents, tools and checklists that you'll need to hit the ground running. You will also have access to our private online community. Visit **www.amyb.com/courses** for details.

Speaking and Webinars

Amy shares relatable and down to earth content including actionable best practices her audience can use right away. To inquire about a possible speaking engagement, speaking topics, and online webinar options, please contact Amy at **www.amyb.com/speaking** for more information.

Workshops

Amy delivers her complete listing and buying courses in a live, 2-day immersive workshop, allowing your group to walk away specialists, armed with every tool and system needed. Graduates receive a Certificate of Achievement, earn a designation, and have access to our exclusive online community of buyer and listing specialists. Ongoing support or remote training can also be designed for your organization. Visit **www.amyb.com/workshops** for details.

Want More Playbook?

For a complete set of tools and resources to help you implement the concepts from *the Playbook for Success*, please visit us at **www.amyb.com/playbook**.

Keep in touch!
#playbookforsuccess

Watch my videos and interviews:
https://www.amyb.com/youtube

Connect On LinkedIn:
https://amyb.com/linkedin

Connect On Facebook:
https://amyb.com/facebook
https://amyb.com/fb-biz

Connect On Instagram:
https://amyb.com/ig